How Business Owners Make More Money And Have More Time

Joe Siecinski

Publishing, production, and editing by Valenzuela Press.

This publication is designed to provide accurate and authoritative information in regard to the subject matters covered. It is sold with the understanding that the author is not engaged in rendering legal, accounting, or similar professional services. If legal advice or other expert assistance is required, the services of a competent professional should be sought.

ISBN: 0615976948

ISBN-13: 978-0615976945

DEDICATION

To my beautiful wife, Lynnette Vedder.

To my son, Garrett Siecinski.

To schedule a free consultation with Joe, go to BrainshareByJoe.com.

To request more copies of this book, or to get printed or digital copies of the worksheets and planners presented in this book, go to BrainshareByJoe.com

Table of Contents

Chapter 1

Introduction

Hi, I'm Joe Siecinski. Thanks for picking up my book.

I help business owners like you make more money and have more time, even if you feel burned out or stuck in your business, and even if you need more sales quickly.

If you feel stuck or burned out or frustrated, believe me. I know what it's like to be there. I was there not too long ago.

Up until 2008, I worked for a Fortune 50 company, running a $250-million global operation. By most measures, I had a phenomenal and very successful career. My plan was to save up and buy an island after I retired.

Retirement came around in 2008. At that time, my investments weren't worth as much as I anticipated. Also around that time, my son wasn't doing so well.

So, long story short, I decided to take a year and a half off to stay home with my son and reflect on my life and what I wanted to do next.

As I was reflecting, I saw so many businesses crash and burn. Not because the business owners weren't smart, because there were some brilliant people who had amazing technology that was five to ten years ahead of today's state-of-the-art technology. Their businesses failed because they didn't have the skills of running a business. I have seen too many small business owners fail just because they get tired and they burn out, and it's because they don't know how to run a business. A baker is good at baking, a scientist is good at inventing new things, but they don't know how to run a business. A big piece of that is sales and marketing, yes. But another part of it is the mindset. And after seeing all these businesses fail, I figured I could help them. I decided to start my own business coaching firm.

While I was starting, I had that same enthusiasm and "go-getter" attitude we all have when we start fresh into the world of being an entrepreneur. And then, after six months of immense struggle and worry, I was in my office at 2 AM, crying my eyes out because my coaching business was failing. I thought I would be able to help other people succeed in business, but I wasn't even doing it for myself! It was a very humbling moment for me, and I worried for the future of my family.

I was crashing and burning. I was ready to give up. Fortunately though, I didn't give up. I kept trying and working to build my business. I faced a lot of struggles and trials for another year. And at the year and a half mark, I was ready to call it quits. I wasn't being successful, and I was afraid I would experience the same end that thousands of other entrepreneurs faced before me. I didn't want to be a statistic.

I knew I was smart. During my career with a Fortune 50 company, I ran a huge global operation. I had experience in sales, marketing, hiring, firing, management, operations, delivery systems... You name a field in a business, and I had been there and done that. So why was I struggling?

Then one day I called my coach, and I soon learned why. I discovered why I was struggling. He showed me why I was feeling burned out, why I was constantly frustrated, and why I felt like throwing in the towel. I simply was lacking the systems, tools, processes, and training to build my business. I just needed a road map.

It's like I was wandering around, trying a bunch of things, not really knowing if each decision I made would help me or hurt me.

My coach helped me tremendously. He told me,

"Hey, you've got so much time to grow your business, you just don't know how to use it." So together, my coach and I came up with the beginning of my Small Business Calendaring System, which is what you're going to learn about in this book.

He told me, "You're thinking wrong. What do we need to think about in our specific space and time?"

So I went to Neuro-Linguistic Programing (NLP) practitioner training to learn more about how the brain works, and how we can use the brain more effectively.

From there, my business started growing. I knew marketing, now I started to do it in the right way in the right time with the right mindset. I knew the sales, now I started doing it right. I knew how to run financial data and how to coach, now I was just doing it with the right mindset in the right time.

It was at this point that my clients were starting to see much more success.

Now, presently in my life and in my business, I can say that I work when I want, where I want. My business provides me with the income I want, and I feel like I can take a vacation whenever I feel like it. Yes, it really is possible for you to experience the same levels of freedom. Many of my current and past clients didn't know if they could achieve it, but after working with me, they are glad they thought it was at least possible and gave it a try.

From my experience, and from the experience of all

of my clients, there are really only three keys to building a successful business. They are:

1. Knowing what to do.

2. Having the right mindset.

3. Allocating the right amount of time for the right actions while in the right mindset.

My goal for this book is to give you those three keys. I want to share with you the exact system I use for my own business and the system I use for my clients to help them make more money and work less. You might be thinking it isn't possible for you. To paraphrase Henry Ford, "If you think you can do a thing or think you can't do a thing, you're right."

Also, throughout this book, you may be tempted to say, "Oh, I knew that already." When you say or think, "I know," your brain shuts off and you can't learn from what you experience. Throughout this book, you may think or say, "I know that." Did you really internalize it? Do you act upon it? Do you do it? Because knowing is not enough, especially as a business owner. Instead, whenever you think, "I know that," change your words to, "Isn't that interesting?" When you say, "Isn't that interesting," you can almost feel your mind staying open to learning and absorbing useful ideas and concepts. That's what I want to do with this book, is open your eyes to the possibilities that you really can have a business that supports the life you want to live.

Isn't that interesting!

I have seen too many business owners' dreams and visions fade, vanish or just become a nightmare. As a business owner, I know what it is like to worry about the day-to-day survival of the business and taking care of my family. I have put in long hours and wondered, "What happened to the dreams and vision I had... What happened to the business that I dreamed about when I started this company?"

I have 3 decades of accomplishment-laden experience and have helped over 2000 companies worldwide to improve their lives and businesses. I use tested and proven systems, tools, and processes. We will plan and execute the tactics to reach your goals. Guaranteed.

Joe Siecinski

Chapter 2

The Reality Of Business

A lot of business owners think business is just common sense. If I have common sense and a will to succeed, I'll be just fine.

That thinking is WRONG. Business is not just common sense. Want proof?

"Of the small businesses that fail, 90% do so because of a lack of skills and knowledge on the part of the owner." - Dunn and Bradstreet

It isn't because of the economy, it isn't because of whatever else. It's because of lack of skills and knowledge on the part of the owner.

"In 70% of small business failures, a key factor was the owner not recognizing or ignoring weaknesses and then not seeking help." - S.C.O.R.E.

And depending on which statistics and industries you analyze, anywhere from 65% - 96% of businesses never make it to their tenth year in business.

So the fact that most businesses don't survive, and most business owners think that all it takes to succeed in business is common sense and the willingness to succeed is proof that business is not just common sense. It's actually very uncommon sense.

And of those businesses that do survive, the overwhelming majority of those are simply glorified jobs. Almost all small businesses don't reach the potential that they could.

Now, if you look at those numbers, the vast majority of businesses fail. It does not have to be that way. There are proven systems, tools and processes that work. There is a path you can walk down to success. However, instead of walking down the path, too many business owners take out their machete and hack through the woods. Not even knowing where they are going or how to get there.

My clients, however, have a path to walk down and we walk it together.

So why do business owners fail? I think part of the problem is our education system in the US. When you go through school, they don't teach you how to run a small business or think like a business owner. A small business owner is not only the CEO, but he has to be the COO, the accountant, the marketing manager, the VP of sales, the human resource representative... There's a lot on your plate as the business owner.

Our educational system teaches you how to be an employee. If you have the narrower, limited scope of responsibility a typical employee does, then the way you learned in school is great. But as the business owner, you have many more hats to wear.

Most businesses that struggle and fail do so because they lack clear goals and an easy-to-follow plan to get there. Many business owners are in a constant state of putting out fires on top of balancing responsibilities, so it's easy to get frustrated and burned out. But that's not what a business is supposed to be. That's not what a business is supposed to do.

So what is business? What is the definition of business? Can you define for me, right now, what a business is?

My definition is: A Commercial, Profitable Enterprise that works without You. If that definition doesn't match your business, you don't have a business. You have a glorified job. And that's OK if that is what you want. However, if you want you don't have to stay trapped in the glorified job that burns you out, you really can have a successful business that gives you more money and more time off in a relatively short amount of time. Your business should work for you, not the other way around. And that's exactly what my clients and I have with our businesses.

Too many business owners treat their businesses like pets. I have to take the dog out for a walk in the morning, take the dog out for a walk at night. Do it every day. It's never going to change. But your business should not be a pet, it should be more like a child. In the beginning, you have to do all the work. But as a child grows, you no longer have to dress your child or cut up your child's food. It should be the same with your business. In the beginning, you have to get it started. But once you reach a certain level, you don't have to do all the work. Then, eventually, the business should take care of you! Wouldn't that be nice?

So what is the purpose of business? The purpose of your business is NOT to provide jobs. It is not to provide security to your employees, and it is not to provide retirements to anyone who just kind of shows up.

There are lots of management theorists, trainers, and academics trying to convince business owners that they should be providing a fun, enjoyable, happy place that's like an amusement park where work occasionally gets done.

These are not the purpose of business. Do you want to provide jobs, and do you want to provide for the well-being of your employees? Do you want your employees to enjoy working for you? Of course, but those things are not the purpose of business.

So what is the purpose of business? The purpose of business is to generate profit for the shareholders. If you own your business, you are the shareholder, and indirectly, maybe your family members are shareholders.

Your first and foremost responsibility and obligation is to manage the business for profit. And in an ideal situation, you do this in a way that doesn't take up all your time. Your business is supposed to work for you, you are not supposed to be trapped or enslaved by the business.

So the definition of business again is a Commercial, Profitable, Enterprise, that works without You. The purpose is to provide you enough money to live life on your own terms. Period. End of story.

So how do you turn your business into a Commercial, Profitable, Enterprise that works without you? How do you build your business to provide you enough money to live life on your own terms?

That is what we're going to outline in the rest of this book, and it starts with the Ownership Mindset.

Joe Siecinski

Chapter 3

Ownership Mindset

When it comes to succeeding in business, there is a line. You can either be above the line, or below the line.

If you are above the line, you take Ownership, Accountability, and Responsibility for everything that happens in your business and your life. Just like the OAR to paddle your way to success. You take ownership of the situation. People who do this have the highest rates of success.

If you are below the line, you have Blame, Excuses or Denial for bad results. You might as well stay in BED. These people tend to have higher rates of failure.

Are you above or below the line?

One day I was giving a presentation on mindset, and one guy in the audience said, "I got mugged, it wasn't my fault."

I said, "Really? Specifically where were you when you got mugged?"

He said, "Los Angeles."

I said, "What time was it when you got mugged?"

He said, "1:30."

I said, "1:30 in the afternoon?"

He said, "No, 1:30 in the morning."

I said, "Hm, isn't that interesting... And specifically what were you doing at that time?"

He said, "I was at the ATM."

I said, "It was 1:30 in the morning in a city you weren't familiar with and you were at the ATM, and it isn't your fault you got mugged?"

He said, "Yeah, I guess I have to take some ownership."

That's right. When we analyze everything, we have some level of responsibility, accountability, or ownership of everything that happens to us and/or how we react when things happen.

So to have your life happen the way you want it to, rather than it just being something that happens to you, you should have written goals. Everyone should have written goals.

The power of planning and written goals...

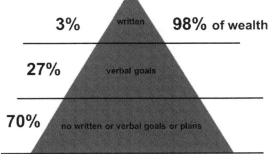

3%   written   98% of wealth

27%   verbal goals

70%   no written or verbal goals or plans

Only 3% of people have written goals and plans, these people account for 98% of the wealth. –Harvard Business School Study

According to a Harvard Business School study, 70% of people have no goals, 27% have verbal goals, and 3% have written goals. Of the 3% who have written goals, 98% of wealth resided in those top 3%. Isn't that interesting?

In my work with business owners, I've come up with a formula for change. This is really where my engineering degree comes in handy.

Your Dissatisfaction times your Vision plus your First Steps must be greater than your Resistance.

If your dissatisfaction or your vision is a 1 or a 0, you probably aren't going to change your situation much. If your resistance to new ideas is high, it's going to take a lot to change your situation.

The Formula for CHANGE ...

$$(D \times V) + F > R$$

Dis-satisfaction
Vision
First Steps
Resistance

So let's talk about some goals. Here are some example goals.

One of my clients had a goal of buying a house. I

asked him, how big is the house? Where is it? What does it look like? How many square feet?

So this client and I came up with a plan. He wants a 5-bedroom, 3-bathroom house, 2500 square feet on a 10,000 square feet lot no more than five miles from the beach and no more than 3 miles from his office by December 31st, 2014. We know it will cost $1.4 million, and he has to make $X per month or year to cover the mortgage. Now we can start putting a plan in place to achieve that goal.

So many business owners never clearly define the goal, so it's really difficult to put a plan in place to get there.

The clearer and more specific the goal, the better your chances of achieving it.

I hear all the time, "I want to make more money." How much more money? What is your specific target?

Your goals must be SMART goals. They must be Specific, Measurable, Achievable, Results-oriented or Realistic, with a Time frame.

So if you want to make $400,000 a year, fantastic! Now we know based on your profit margins, what your gross revenue has to be. We divide that target gross revenue amount by your average transaction size, now we have the number of sales we have to make. Once we know how many sales you need to make, we can determine how many prospects you have to go after, and how many prospects and sales you need each quarter, month, week, day, and hour.

So ask yourself, how much do you want to make per year? How many vacations do you want to take? What time do you want to be home everyday? How many hours do you want to work per week? Once you get clear on what you want, we can work on creating your plan to get there. And in order to do the things necessary to make the plan happen, first you need time.

Once we have the goal, we then determine what we need to do, then who we need to be to do what we need to do to have what we want to have.

BE X DO = HAVE

Your Twelve Month Goals For Your Business

S = Specific   M = Measurable   A = Achievable   R = Results-Oriented   T = Time-Framed

GOAL	WHAT DO I HAVE TO DO TO ACHIEVE THE GOAL?	WHO DO I HAVE TO BE TO GET THERE?
1.		
2.		
3.		
4.		
5.		
6.		

Joe Siecinski

Chapter 4

Your Calendar

What is the #1 reason for business failure? Burnout. Lots of business owners say it's lack of capital or lack of something else, but in my experience, burnout is a huge problem for most business owners. They run so hard, so fast, for so long, until one day they just say, "I'm done!" It's like being the mouse on the wheel running around and around and around.

I hear people saying all the time that they don't have enough time or money, they feel scatter-brained, they have trouble sleeping, my business is failing...

I hear a lot of business owners say, "I can't get my operations to run without me." This is a big one because the owner knows how to do it, but the owner lacks the systems and tools to train someone else to do the work.

The Small Business Calendaring System enables you to resolve all of these things. It relieves you from burnout, time pressure, and brain scatter. It enables business success. It allows you to allocate your time or employee productivity. You can finally get your operations to work without you having to do all the work.

The goal of the Small Business Calendaring System is to give you eight more hours in your business week, without having to spend eight more hours at the physical location of your business. Then, once we have time, we can address all of the other issues. We can address sales, marketing, operations, hiring, firing, training, finances, and whatever other issues you might be facing.

Most business owners say, "I don't have time for that." You're right, you don't. Let's get your time back, then we can work on your destination and what we have to do to get you there. We can work on your team, your delivery, your money, your niche, hiring people, and everything else that looks like a big mess on your plate but looks nice and organized when you break it down.

The business owners who come to me who have the biggest and fastest successes are the ones who tell me, "Hey, I don't know everything, I could use some help." My clients who succeed get there because they are open to learning and implementing new things.

The business owners who fail normally have attitudes of, "Oh, I don't need your help. Your advice doesn't apply to me." When something is suggested to them, they might respond with, "Well, we shouldn't do that because we've never done it that way before." Well, I know you haven't done it that way before, because if you had, you wouldn't be talking to me right now asking for help!

So it's really important you keep your mind open to this calendaring strategy.

My job isn't to give you fish, but to teach you how to fish. And when you are done with my program, you'll not only be able to run your business, but you can run any business you want.

Richard Branson is one of my favorite role models. He is an living example of the saying, "If you can run one business you can run a hundred." That's true. In our system, we take some of the best strategies and methods used by the top entrepreneurs around, and we use these techniques to help you manage and grow your business.

Joe Siecinski

Chapter 5

Brainshare For Your Business

If your brain is operations and you are trying to do marketing, you're going to fail.

If you're in sales mode and you are trying to do finances, you're going to have trouble.

When you are in marketing mode, be in marketing mode and know your roles and responsibilities.

Every business should have an organizational chart to know your roles and responsibilities, even if you are a solo entrepreneur. The reason for that is when you are in your marketing role, you know what your metrics are and you can align to those metrics.

Marketing metrics are generally lead generation. How many leads are you getting in a given time frame?

ORGANIZATION CHART:

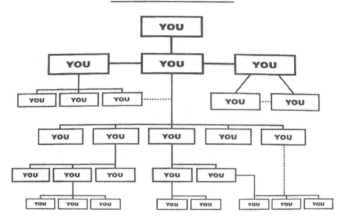

If you're in the mindset of making the sale and you're doing marketing, you are going to struggle. Isn't that interesting?

When you're in marketing mode, stay in marketing mode. When you're in sales mode, don't think about how you are going to deliver that service. Stay in sales mode. When you're in sales mode, it's all about conversion rate.

When you're in delivery mode, it's all about delivering in the most effective and efficient way that also keeps the customer happy so they buy more.

Position Description

Please complete the following form for your current position.

Job title: _____

Your name: _____

Brief description and general overview of position:

_____
_____
_____

Position responsible to: _____
(who do you report to and what is their position?)

Key tasks

Describe key tasks	Indicate % of total time spent on these tasks

Key performance indicators

Evaluation criteria	Target
eg average margin on sales	30%

Skills required

_____
_____
_____
_____
_____

Desirable personal qualities

_____
_____
_____
_____

Recommended training for your position

_____
_____
_____

Completed training (from the list above, what have you already completed?)

_____
_____
_____

Suggestions to improve the enjoyment and/or efficiency in your work

_____
_____
_____
_____
_____
_____
_____

Signed _____

Date completed _____ / ____ / _____

When you're in CFO mode, you're running reports and looking at budgets and looking at the numbers, and it's a very analytical mode. Stay in that mode. When you're in HR mode, it's about hiring, firing, and training.

When you're in CEO mode, it's about strategic direction. It's about managing the other functions and deciding your goals and benchmarks for the future.

Single-person businesses have to be a little

schizophrenic. I'll be here in my office and say, "Okay everyone, company meeting!" and it's just me.

I'll say, "Okay, CFO, what do the numbers look like?"

"Hey Mr. CEO, we kept our costs under control. so we hit profit percentages but we didn't hit revenue numbers."

"Why didn't we hit revenue numbers?"

"Hey, I'm just financial, talk to sales."

"VP of sales, why didn't we hit our numbers?"

"Our conversion rate was 38%, our goal was 35%. We hit our numbers, talk to marketing."

"Hey Chief Marketing Officer, why didn't we hit out lead numbers?"

"Well Mr. CEO, I didn't get the hours and budget I needed to generate the leads we needed."

"What do you need so we hit our lead numbers next month?"

"I need two more hours of time and $1,000 to put into marketing."

"CFO, do we have the money to cover that?"

"We sure do."

"Great. Marketing, you got your two hours and your

money. Can we hit our lead numbers next month?"

"Yes we can."

"Great. Good meeting everyone."

And that's the CEO's job. Strategic direction and managing the other functions. Isn't that interesting?

Chapter 6

Organizing Your Time

So now we're going to plan our time.

"But I don't have time to plan, Joe." If you don't have time to plan it, you won't have time to do it. People spend more time planning their wedding than they spend planning their lives. It doesn't take long. Fifteen minutes at the start of your day, twenty at the end of the day is all it takes. Depending on which survey you look at, the average person in the US over the age of 2 spends 15-32 hours per week watching television. Even if you were to just plan during commercials, you would have time to plan your day, your business, and your week. If you're unwilling to even do that, then your dissatisfaction and your vision don't outweigh your resistance. You're going to continue being stuck where you are.

Every task you do falls into one of four categories:

1. Important and urgent

2. Not important and urgent

3. Important and not urgent

4. Not important and not urgent

	Urgent	Not Urgent
Important	**I** (MANAGE) • Crisis • Medical emergencies • Pressing problems • Deadline-driven projects • Last-minute preparations for scheduled activities **Quadrant of Necessity**	**II** (FOCUS) • Preparation/planning • Prevention • Values clarification • Exercise • Relationship-building • True recreation/relaxation **Quadrant of Quality & Personal Leadership**
Not Important	**III** (AVOID) • Interruptions, some calls • Some mail & reports • Some meetings • Many "pressing" matters • Many popular activities **Quadrant of Deception**	**IV** (AVOID) • Trivia, busywork • Junk mail • Some phone messages/email • Time wasters • Escape activities • Viewing mindless TV shows **Quadrant of Waste**

(Concept developed by Steven Covey)

Your goal is to get rid of as many not important tasks as possible. You want to spend time on things that are important but not urgent, because these tend to have the biggest payoff. You're going to get the important and urgent ones done because they are important and urgent. The important and not urgent ones are the tasks that require focus.

To get going with your calendar, you need to have "imperatives." Here are some sample imperatives:

There are 40 hours in a work week. You work to enjoy life, work is not supposed to consume your life.

This is your calendar; you control it, it does not control you! Stuff happens, adjust your calendar to it.

"Yeah, but Joe, I work 60 hours, I work 30 hours." This is a guideline, this isn't written in stone.

Set any imperatives you like. It could be you doing only a certain type of task on certain days, you working only a certain number of hours per week, you only working certain days, you taking every Wednesday afternoon off, etc. Do what fits your life and business.

So our starting point to developing your calendar is to categorize your business into its main functions. Every business is unique, so your categories may be different. Look at your organizational chart. If you don't have an organizational chart, that's a red flag. You should create one(see previous example)

Most businesses have these areas:

- Marketing – lead generation

- Sales – conversion rate

- Operations – anything related to delivery, including administrative work

- Finance – accounting and reporting

- CEO – strategic direction and review of all other functions

- Travel – self-explanatory, but takes up more time than you would think

Your business may have more or different areas, but these are where we are going to focus for the demonstration in this book.

Now, let's break down your time allocations.

- Marketing – 30% of your 40 hours = 12 hours

- Sales – 20% of your 40 hours = 8 hours

- Operations – 30% of your 40 hours = 12 hours

- Finance – 5% of your 40 hours = 2 hours

- CEO – 10% of your 40 hours = 4 hours

- Travel – 5% of your 40 hours = 2 hours

These numbers may change depending on your business. If you are starting up new, you probably don't have much delivery or operations to do, you can move some of the time to marketing and sales. Review these time allocations at least quarterly, some do monthly.

So for your business specifically, what should you be doing to get where you want to go? Not what are you doing now, but what should you be doing?

Sales	Marketing	Operations	Finance	CEO	Travel
%	%	%	%	%	%
Hrs	Hrs	Hrs	Hrs	Hrs	Hrs

Marketing	Sales	Operations	Finance	CEO	Travel
30%	20 %	30%	5%	10%	5%
12Hrs	8Hrs	12Hrs	2Hrs	4Hrs	2Hrs

Calendaring System

Time	Sunday 24-Jun-12	Monday 25-Jun-12	Tuesday 26-Jun-12
7:00 AM to 7:30 AM			
7:30 AM to 8:00 AM			
8:00 AM to 8:15 AM			
8:15 AM to 8:30 AM			
8:30 AM to 8:45 AM			
8:45 AM to 9:00 AM			
9:00 AM to 9:15 AM			
9:15 AM to 9:30 AM			
9:30 AM to 9:45 AM			
9:45 AM to 10:00 AM			
10:00 AM to 10:15 AM			
10:15 AM to 10:30 AM			
10:30 AM to 10:45 AM			
10:45 AM to 11:00 AM			
11:00 AM to 11:15 AM			
11:15 AM to 11:30 AM			
11:30 AM to 11:45 AM			
11:45 AM to 12:00 PM			
12:00 PM to 12:45 PM			
1:00 PM to 1:15 PM			
1:15 PM to 1:30 PM			
1:30 PM to 1:45 PM			
1:45 PM to 2:00 PM			
2:00 PM to 2:15 PM			
2:15 PM to 2:30 PM			
2:30 PM to 2:45 PM			
2:45 PM to 3:00 PM			
3:00 PM to 3:15 PM			
3:15 PM to 3:30 PM			
3:30 PM to 3:45 PM			
3:45 PM to 4:00 PM			
4:00 PM to 4:15 PM			
4:15 PM to 4:30 PM			
4:30 PM to 4:45 PM			
4:45 PM to 5:00 PM			
EVENING ACTIVITIES			

BOLD TYPE

Company Name

Wednesday	Thursday	Friday	Saturday
27-Jun-12	28-Jun-12	29-Jun-12	30-Jun-12

Now, list out all the tasks you have to do in a given week. Categorize them. Group your marketing tasks together, your sales tasks together, etc. Plug these tasks in to your major time categories. Give yourself 15 minutes per task if needed.

Most business owners have forty to sixty tasks per week that need to get done. That leaves one hundred 15-minute time slots, which is about 25 hours. Isn't that interesting?

As we start plugging these tasks in, we'll find out that some of these tasks take longer than 15 minutes. That's okay, just break your tasks into 15-minute chunks and plug them in (see examples on pages 44 and 45).

Now, we have time to do everything else we have to do to build the business. Now we have time to do hire new staff, train employees, develop standard operating procedures, and do more marketing. Isn't that interesting?

Plug in these tasks in the time blocks in your weekly calendar.

As you build out your new weekly calendar, here are three keys you'll need to ensure that this approach works for you:

1. Start your day with 15 minutes. Review what you have to do that day and what your goals are.

2. End the day with at least 20 minutes. Review the day and rate it on a scale of 1 to 10. If it's an 8 or below,

what do you need to make it a 10? Plan out the next day, including anything you didn't get done during the day earlier. If you are worried about something then schedule time to worry about it. This will let your subconscious mind work on it while you sleep and free up your conscious mind.

3. Put buffers in your day. Take a couple of breaks during the day to allow your brain time to switch from CEO mode to CMO mode or CFO mode. These also act as shock absorbers. If you had a rough morning, these allow you to get back on track to do what you have to do during the afternoon.

This is what your calendar should look like (see pages 42 and 43), blocked for major functions. I recommend color-coding your major functions.

I recommend blocking off time for your major functions, scheduling 45 minutes to an hour for each major function of your business. Block off time to do emails. Block off time for meetings or phone calls, and group them together.

To see what a completed calendar looks like with the tasks and activities plugged in to the major function time blocks, see the calendar on pages 44 and 45.

It might take a few tries to get your calendar just right. Try it for a few weeks, then review it. Tweak it as you go along. Still, having a calendar to manage your time is better than not having a system at all. Isn't that interesting?

Default Diary

Coach Schedule	Sunday	Monday	Tuesday
Time			
7:00 AM to 7:30 AM	Personal	Personal Time	Personal Time
7:30 AM to 8:00 AM			
8:00 AM to 8:15 AM			
8:15 AM to 8:30 AM			
8:30 AM to 8:45 AM		Plan Daily Activities	Plan Daily Activities
8:45 AM to 9:00 AM		Email	Email
9:00 AM to 9:15 AM		Marketing	Sales
9:15 AM to 9:30 AM		Marketing	Sales
9:30 AM to 9:45 AM		Marketing	Sales
9:45 AM to 10:00 AM		Marketing	Sales
10:00 AM to 10:15 AM		Marketing	Sales
10:15 AM to 10:30 AM		Break	Break
10:30 AM to 10:45 AM		Sales	Marketing
10:45 AM to 11:00 AM		Sales	Marketing
11:00 AM to 11:15 AM		Sales	Marketing
11:15 AM to 11:30 AM		Sales	Marketing
11:30 AM to 11:45 AM		Sales	Marketing
11:45 AM to 12:00 PM		Email	Email
12:00 PM to		Lunch	Lunch
to 1:00 PM			
1:00 PM to 1:15 PM		Marketing	Travel
1:15 PM to 1:30 PM		Marketing	Travel
1:30 PM to 1:45 PM		Marketing	Sales
1:45 PM to 2:00 PM		Marketing	Sales
2:00 PM to 2:15 PM		Marketing	Sales
2:15 PM to 2:30 PM		Marketing	Sales
2:30 PM to 2:45 PM		Marketing	Sales
2:45 PM to 3:00 PM		Break	Break
3:00 PM to 3:15 PM		Sales	Operations
3:15 PM to 3:30 PM		Sales	Operations
3:30 PM to 3:45 PM		Sales	Operations
3:45 PM to 4:00 PM		Sales	Operations
4:00 PM to 4:15 PM		Sales	Operations
4:15 PM to 4:30 PM		Email	Email
4:30 PM to 4:45 PM		Travel	Operations
4:45 PM to 5:00 PM		Sales	Operations
5:00 PM to 5:15 PM		Sales	Operations
5:15 PM to 5:30 PM		Sales	Operations
5:30 PM to 5:45 PM		Sales	Operations
5:45 PM to 6:00 PM		Email	Email
EVENING ACTIVITIES		Review Day and rate it from 1-10. What would get i

Sales
Marketing
Operations
Finance
CEO
Travel
Personal

XYZ Company

Wednesday	Thursday	Friday	Saturday
Personal Time	Personal Time	Personal Time	Personal
Plan Daily Activities	Plan Daily Activities	Plan Daily Activities	
Email	Email	Email	
Marketing	Marketing	Finance	
Marketing	Marketing	Finance	
Marketing	Marketing	Finance	
Marketing	Marketing	Finance	
Marketing	Marketing	Finance	
Break	Break	Break	
Operations	Travel	CEO	
Operations	Sales	CEO	
Operations	Sales	CEO	
Operations	Sales	CEO	
Operations	Sales	CEO	
Email	Sales	Email	
Lunch	Lunch	Lunch	
Marketing	Email	Email	
Marketing	Operations	CEO	
Marketing	Operations	CEO	
Marketing	Operations	CEO	
Marketing	Operations	CEO	
Marketing	Operations	CEO	
Marketing	Operations	CEO	
Break	Break	Break	
Operations	Marketing	Finance	
Operations	Marketing	Finance	
Operations	Marketing	Finance	
Operations	Marketing	CEO	
Operations	Marketing	CEO	
Email	Email	Email	
Marketing	Sales	Marketing	
Marketing	Sales	Marketing	
Marketing	Sales	Marketing	
Marketing	Sales	Marketing	
Operations	Sales	Marketing	
Email	Email	Email	
closer to 10? Define Challenges and Schedule time to work on them.			

Sales
Marketing
Operations
Finance
CEO
Travel
Personal

Default Diary

Coach Schedule			Sunday	Monday	Tuesday
Time					
7:00 AM	to	7:30 AM	Personal	**Personal Time**	**Personal Time**
7:30 AM	to	8:00 AM			
8:00 AM	to	8:15 AM			
8:15 AM	to	8:30 AM			
8:30 AM	to	8:45 AM		**Plan Daily Activities**	**Plan Daily Activities**
8:45 AM	to	9:00 AM		**Email**	**Email**
9:00 AM	to	9:15 AM		Marketing Plan Review	Review sales plan
9:15 AM	to	9:30 AM		Marketing Activities Sheet Rev	Review sales plan
9:30 AM	to	9:45 AM		Marketing Activity #1	Review sales plan
9:45 AM	to	10:00 AM		Marketing Activity #1	Funnel Review
10:00 AM	to	10:15 AM		Marketing Activity #1	Funnel Review
10:15 AM	to	10:30 AM		**Break**	**Break**
10:30 AM	to	10:45 AM		Work Leads from Marketing	Marketing Activity #2
10:45 AM	to	11:00 AM		Work Leads from Marketing	Marketing Activity #2
11:00 AM	to	11:15 AM		Work Leads from Marketing	Marketing Activity #2
11:15 AM	to	11:30 AM		Work Leads from Marketing	Marketing Activity #2
11:30 AM	to	11:45 AM		Work Leads from Marketing	Marketing Activity #2
11:45 AM	to	12:00 PM		**Email**	**Email**
12:00 PM	to			**Lunch**	**Lunch**
	to	1:00 PM			
1:00 PM	to	1:15 PM		Marketing Activity #1	Travel
1:15 PM	to	1:30 PM		Marketing Activity #1	Travel
1:30 PM	to	1:45 PM		Marketing Activity #1	F2F sales
1:45 PM	to	2:00 PM		Marketing Activity #1	F2F sales
2:00 PM	to	2:15 PM		Marketing Activity #1	F2F sales
2:15 PM	to	2:30 PM		Marketing Activity #1	F2F sales
2:30 PM	to	2:45 PM		Marketing Activity #1	F2F sales
2:45 PM	to	3:00 PM		**Break**	**Break**
3:00 PM	to	3:15 PM		Sales Cold Calls	Operations
3:15 PM	to	3:30 PM		Sales Cold Calls	Operations
3:30 PM	to	3:45 PM		Sales Cold Calls	Operations
3:45 PM	to	4:00 PM		Sales Cold Calls	Operations
4:00 PM	to	4:15 PM		Sales Cold Calls	Operations
4:15 PM	to	4:30 PM		**Email**	**Email**
4:30 PM	to	4:45 PM		Travel	Operations
4:45 PM	to	5:00 PM		F2F sales	Operations
5:00 PM	to	5:15 PM		F2F sales	Operations
5:15 PM	to	5:30 PM		F2F sales	Operations
5:30 PM	to	5:45 PM		F2F sales	Operations
5:45 PM	to	6:00 PM		**Email**	**Email**
EVENING ACTIVITIES					
				Review Day and rate it from 1-10. What would g
				Sales	
				Marketing	
				Operations	
				Finance	
				CEO	
				Travel	
				Personal	

XYZ Company

Wednesday	Thursday	Friday	Saturday
Personal Time	Personal Time	Personal Time	Personal
Plan Daily Activities	Plan Daily Activities	Plan Daily Activities	
Email	Email	Email	
Marketing Activity #2	Marketing Activity #4	Finance Book keeping	
Marketing Activity #2	Marketing Activity #4	Finance Book keeping	
Marketing Activity #2	Marketing Activity #4	Finance Book keeping	
Marketing Activity #2	Marketing Activity #4	Finance Book keeping	
Marketing Activity #2	Marketing Activity #4	Finance Book keeping	
Break	Break	Break	
Operations	Travel	CEO Sales Review	
Operations	F2F sales	CEO Marketing Review	
Operations	F2F sales	CEO Finance Review	
Operations	F2F sales	CEO operations Review	
Operations	F2F sales	CEO Company Report	
Email	F2F sales	Email	
Lunch	Lunch	Lunch	
Marketing Activity #3	EMail	Email	
Marketing Activity #3	Operations	CEO Sales Plan	
Marketing Activity #3	Operations	CEO Marketing Plan	
Marketing Activity #3	Operations	CEO Finance Plan	
Marketing Activity #3	Operations	CEO operations Plan	
Marketing Activity #3	Operations	CEO Company Overall Plan	
Marketing Activity #3	Operations	CEO Stategy	
Break	Break	Break	
Operations	Marketing Activity #5	P/L Reports	
Operations	Marketing Activity #5	P/L Reports	
Operations	Marketing Activity #5	P/L Reports	
Operations	Marketing Activity #5	CEO Stategy	
Operations	Marketing Activity #5	CEO Stategy	
Email	Email	Email	
Marketing Activity #3	Sales Followups Phone	Review Marketing Results	
Marketing Activity #3	Sales Followups Phone	Review Marketing Results	
Marketing Activity #3	Review Sales Results	Plan Marketing Activities	
Marketing Activity #3	Review Sales Results	Plan Marketing Activities	
Operations	Review Sales Results	Plan Marketing Activities	
Email	Email	Email	
et it closer to 10? Define Challenges and Schedule time to work on them.			

		Sales	
		Marketing	
		Operations	
		Finance	
		CEO	
		Travel	
		Personal	

Joe Siecinski

Chapter 7

Clarifying Marketing

When I'm working with my coaching clients, we start with setting up your calendar. Then, we go into doing something with your marketing time so you get in the habit of doing it. Then we'll do the strategic marketing plan to get you doing the best marketing strategies. The reason I do it this way is because I've spent so much time working with clients starting with the strategic marketing plan then going to the tactical marketing plan, but there's no time in the calendar to do anything. So we start with the calendar first so we can clear up time for you to do something, then doing the right things. It may seem a little backwards, but it works for my clients. Let's continue on from the calendar and go into tactical marketing.

Now we've got the template and we've got some time allocations for our major functions scheduled out.

So what do we do in our marketing time? Most small businesses that I work with struggle with marketing, so we want to start with a marketing plan. I recommend starting with a tactical marketing plan. We're going to walk through a few examples.

	Activity 1	Activity 2	Activity 3	Activity 4	Activity 5
WHO: are your target market – specifically must be 10 or less					
WHAT: will you offer them (product/service)					
WHY: would they buy from you					
HOW: will you get your offer to them					
WHEN: exactly when will you do this					
INVESTMENT: What resources will it need					
OUTCOME: what is your desired outcome					

As you see on the marketing planning document, there is room for five activities. Typically, I recommend one activity a day for the week. Or, if you want, you can do one activity a week and you can use the planning document for the month, depending on what your strategic marketing plan is (we'll get into the strategic marketing plan later). For now, we're talking marketing tactics and what you should do with your marketing time slots.

One of the hardest thing for business owners to do is develop who is their target market specifically. This is a hard thing to grasp sometimes. But if you look at the graph, you see it says, "Specifically, who is your target?" It must be ten or less. I ask my clients to write down ten people's names that are in their target market, or ten company names that are in their target market. Once we have it down to 10 or less, you can now go and do something with that. If you have more than 10, you start procrastinating. Or you start saying, "Oh well, let me do an email blast to 5,000 people." Which could be an activity, but you aren't really targeted then.

So we're not saying that these are the ONLY 10 people we are targeting. If you target ten people today in your marketing time, then you contact ten more tomorrow, then you have targeted 50 potential customers or clients by the end of the week. These are people you ACTUALLY targeted, reached out to, and talked to. Big difference between calling someone or showing up in person and just putting up a billboard or sending a flier that goes straight to the trash can. And now we can actually do something with that. Does that make sense? Isn't that interesting?

So what you do depends on your strategic marketing plan and what your time allocations are. These are all just tools for your business. Every business is unique. These are just tools. They can be modified or adjusted any way you find appropriate for your business.

You know your business better than anyone else.

For example, let's start with Marketing Activity 1, in the first column of the marketing planning document. Let's say it's a fitness center. So this fitness center wants to target specifically professional golfers. So we go get a list of professional golfers in your specific geographic area, and we write down their names. Now we know who they are. Now what do we want to offer them?

Every business is different, you've got to find out what it is you're going to offer them. Can I offer them a free consultation? Can I offer them a report on "how to improve your game by 2 strokes?" Can I teach them how to remove pain from their golf game? There are so many things you can offer them. If you don't know what you're going to offer to your target audience to get them to call you or visit your place of business, you and I will walk through this together to figure out what you can offer your target market.

Why would they buy it from you? What makes you better, what makes you different? Why should I take a lesson at your facility rather than a different facility? Why should I take your classes instead of other classes? Maybe you have some educational background that speaks to your skills. Maybe you have helped hundreds of golfers overcome back pain from playing. Something along those lines.

Now how are you going to give them the offer? Are you going to call? Are you going to send a letter or a postcard? Are you going to knock on their door? Are you going to send a flier? Are you going to send a singing telegram? Are you going to call-mail-call? (Call and say, "I have something for you," send it, then call, "Hey I wanted to make sure you got it.")

Next is, "When specifically are you going to do this?" This is when you pull out your calendar and you actually allocate the time to do that activity or the steps in that activity that need to get accomplished to get the activity done.

For example: if you're going to do a flier, first you need to draft the flier. If you are making phone calls, plug in time to call. If you're going to send a letter, you have to write, design, and send out the mail pieces.

This is where the marketing plan and the calendar tie together.

Next is, what is your investment? How much is it going to cost you? Two hours of time, an hour of time, some amount of money, a box of golf balls with your logo, if you're driving to visit and it takes $3 of gasoline. Tally up the total investment, including your time. Every business owner's time is worth at least $100 per hour.

And what is the outcome? Since this is a marketing plan, the outcome is not a client or a sale. The outcome is typically a phone conversation, a face-to-face meeting, or a proposal. Typical numbers are if you're targeting 10, and assuming a 10% conversion rate, that would give you 1 face-to-face or 1 proposal or 1 teleconference or 1 next step in the sales process. This is how you go through your marketing plan to start generating your leads or to get to the next step of making a sale.

Then the next day, do the next activity. Say you're doing a networking event. Who specifically at that networking event do you want to target? What will you offer them? Why would they choose you? How will you get them your message? If you're at a networking event, you're probably going to walk up to them and hand them your card and try to schedule some time. When are you going to do it? What's the investment? What's the outcome?

Let's say another one of your activities is social media. Who specifically is your target? Write down a couple of names of who you're trying to target with that status update or with that blog post. Then what are you going to offer? Why would they buy it from you? How are you going to deliver the offer? Facebook post, Facebook ad, Linkedin post or Linkedin ad, post it in Linkedin groups, post to your blog, send out a newsletter, whatever works for you. When are you doing it? Plug in the time allocation into your calendar. What's the investment? Write the article, write the post, some amount of time. What's the outcome? A response, a face-to-face, or something.

You continue through this process and you set up your week's activities. The first time you do this, it typically takes about two hours. After that, these activities and the questions start to become very similar. You'll be able to do your marketing review from the prior week in 15 minutes and you do your marketing plan for the next week in 15 minutes, then you get started.

That's what you do in your marketing time slots as you start moving forward.

Can you have 10 marketing activities instead of 5? Absolutely. It's your business, you know it better than anybody else.

For many of my clients, marketing can seem overwhelming. You may not have known where to start or what to do either, but now you have a clear, easy-to-follow step-by-step plan. This is what you do and this is how you do it, and it doesn't take as long as you would have thought. You have clarity. Now you have something you can go do versus sitting there for two hours thinking about what you're going to do.

Back to our example. I could target Santa Clara golfers and offer them a free golf lesson. I'm going to write an ad in the Santa Clara newspaper. It's going to cost a few hundred dollars, and the outcome I want is four phone calls.

And as a quick note, any time you run an ad in a newspaper or on a flier or a mail piece or a billboard or a postcard or a commercial or an email, have a marketing phone line that you can monitor to measure your results. How many phone calls are coming in on that line? You can use Google phone lines for free, or you can add another phone line for about $15.

If you're interested in 10x10 marketing, question-based selling, sales processes, sales skills, organizational charts, roles and responsibilities, putting together your ultimate team, optimizing your business, give me a call or look out for my other books.

Chapter 8

Your Next Steps

Congratulations, you made it! At this point, you now know how to better manage your time and your business to give you more free time and earn you more money. You have clarity on what your big goals are, and you know how much time to allocate to each of the major areas of your business. You have also heard remarks from a few of my clients.

At this point, you may be interested in getting help from a coach, or you may be wondering if you should work with a coach at all.

So why should I work with a coach? Well, a good coach is kind of like a card catalog in a library. When you go to a library, there are books everywhere with lots of information. If you are looking for something that specifically applies to you, you want to get that information as quickly and easily as you can.

If you need information on the ancient Roman empire, you don't want to wander around wasting a bunch of time, reading books on lizards or how to build a website. You want information about the Roman empire so you can go get done what needs to get done. Same idea with a search engine. Rather than going to every website on the internet to find the information you need, you just type something into a search engine and it gives you the information you wanted, saving you a ton of time, and giving you the very best information on that topic.

Same with a coach. An experienced coach has been there, done that, got the T-shirt. An experienced coach has gone through what you are going through right now. If you are struggling to get more customers, if you feel burned out and trapped in your business, if you can't take a vacation because your business will fail without you... An experienced business coach has gone through many of these exact same issues and came out successful on the other side. Not only that, but an experienced coach has helped many others before you to do the same thing, turning frustration and problems into freedom and relief.

So why should you have a coach? They save you from having to reinvent the wheel. If you wanted to, you could go out and build your own car. You would have to learn about engineering, buy a bunch of materials, do a lot of testing and trial and error, then, eventually, after a lot of time and work, you might put together a car. But guess what? Cars have been around for over a hundred years. No need to build one, you can go buy one and save yourself a lot of time, effort, energy, frustration, and problems if you just go get one that has already been designed by some very qualified engineers!

So you now have a choice to make. If you feel burned out from working hard every day and not feeling like you're getting the payoff, if you feel like you are earning just enough to get by but you could use more money to spend on vacation or savings or the kids, if you are spending too much time on your business and your children are growing up not knowing who you are, you have to decide now. Do you want to continue feeling burned out? Do you want to continue to just "get by"? Do you want to continue to not have time or money for vacation? Do you want to continue spending too much time on your business? Or do you want to make more money and have more freedom, more time to spend with your family, and more satisfaction in your personal and professional life? If you want the second option, you need a qualified coach who can take you there.

Even Olympic athletes, the most successful athletes in the entire world, have coaches. These are the people who run faster, swim faster, and perform better than any other athlete or team in the world. In major league baseball, football, hockey, you name the sport, there is a coach. Why? Because the coach can point the team and the athletes in the right direction, saving them from injury and trouble.

Some people think having a coach is a sign of weakness. "Oh, I don't need a coach! I'll just figure it all out on my own." You're free to do that if you like, but what a waste of time! Imagine if you had to learn how to tie your shoes, drive your car, or read without any direction or help from teachers or parents. I think you get the analogy.

Running a successful business that brings you more money and more freedom is just a matter of learning a skill. If you can tie your shoes right now, you have the ability to learn a skill. That means you can learn and benefit from the coaching of your parents. In a similar way, you can learn the skills of having a successful business. You just need the right tools, systems, and processes to make it work at the highest level with minimal work or effort on your part. That's what a coach can provide you.

"Why do I need a business coach now, Joe?" Well, let me ask you something then. Are you happy with where you are? If nothing changes, are you perfectly happy with your business and the lifestyle you live because of it? And, when is the best time to improve your business, increase your profit, and reduce the amount of time you work?

Chapter 9

How To Choose A Coach

If you are reading this chapter right now, you are probably looking for guidance on how to build your business. That's a very good thing to want.

Before you go select a coach, here are a few questions you should ask. My answers to the questions follow.

Question #1 – Do you have a guarantee? What is it?

My guarantee is that I pay for myself in four months or you get your money back. That means starting no later than month five, you make a profit from the help

I provide you.

Question #2 – How many other businesses have you coached?

I've helped hundreds in a wide range of industries.

Question #3 – What results have your clients seen?

Here are just a few remarks from some of my clients:

Working with Joe has been extremely helpful to my business. Three things stand out: 1) The calendaring system he teaches works. I've tried quite a few and found most to be a burden. This works for me. 2) His ability to pose questions that cause you to look at things from another angle. 3) His sincerity in wanting to help you to be enormously successful. I started as a skeptic. Now I'm a fan.

- Dave Kocharhook, Senior Vice President at Midland American Capital

Joe has been a great coach. After meeting with him for the first time, we put some business strategies together and I had had my best month ever! I look forward to working with Joe in the future. He is knowledgeable, personable and wants to see you grow!

- Jeff R., San Jose, CA

Question #4 – Can I talk to some of your clients?

Sure! Call up any of them and ask them about me.

Or, contact me and I can set up a time where we can jump on a conference call and you can ask them anything you like.

Question #5 – What education or experience do you have in this area where I need help?

I'm a certified business coach and NLP (Neuro-Linguistic Programing) practitioner, I have a degree in engineering and an MBA in marketing. I have done over 2,000 sales calls, giving me a level of understanding in the sales process that helps all of my clients. I managed a global operation for a Fortune 50 company before I retired, and while I was there, I managed sales, marketing, delivery, operations, production, hiring and firing, profit and loss... You name it, I did it.

If you get good answers to these questions, that coach is a good choice. If you don't get answers you like to these questions, pick a different coach. I personally interviewed 10 coaches before I picked mine.

Another word about coaching. Coaching has a questionable reputation for some people. There are no regulations regarding coaching so anyone can hang out a shingle and say, "I am a coach." Ensure your choice has the skills, results, systems, tools, or processes to really help people.

I had two coaches just a few weeks ago come in to my office to get coaching from me, and I sat down with them. I'm helping them with their sales plan, their marketing plan, their financial plan, and I'm asking them. "Are you doing your personality profiles?"

"What's a personality profile?"

"How can you help them if you don't know their personality profile? How can you help if you don't know their learning style? If you don't know how their learn, how can you help your clients learn in the way that's easiest and best for them?" I trained them on DISC and VAK.

There are a lot of coaches out there that aren't really coaches, they're cheerleaders. They just try to give you some rah-rah motivation and wish you the best, but they don't give you the tools, systems, training, or skill set you really need to succeed.

Find one that walks the talk and work with someone who is very reputable and is willing to work with you and guide you in a way that's easiest for you to implement. Your coach should not only motivate you, but give you what you really need to grow your business in the shortest amount of time possible.

My clients want a coach, not a cheerleader. Someone who will work with you one-on-one and give you specific strategies and tools to help your business, not give you a one-size-fits-all generic plan or a bunch of untested, guess-based approaches. This stuff works, and you'll find testimonials from some of my clients later in this book.

Chapter 10

Your Invitation

I hope you learned some valuable techniques. My goal is to help every business I come in contact with, so I hope I accomplished that in our short time together here.

I would like to invite you to take the next step to help you make more money and have more time off. Just contact my office, and I'll set you up with a free consultation. Even if we don't end up working together, my goal is to show you how you can increase your sales and profits and work less at the same time so you have more money and time to spend on family, friends, and fun.

To get started, just visit my site at BrainshareByJoe.com and click the "schedule a free session" link. You can then pick a time that works best for you. You'll get an email confirmation to let you know that your session is scheduled. That's it!

Right now, I'm confident that you are thinking, "Well that was nice, Joe. I got some good ideas, and I'll schedule a conversation with you someday."

I have to caution you against that thinking. Each day you delay contacting me is a day longer you miss out on increased profit and decreased work. Do you want to make more and work less?

I have just a few final questions for you if you don't mind. Read these very closely and carefully consider your answers.

Do you see how my ideas and strategies can help you make more and work less?

Are you interested in making more and working less?

If you were ever going to start making more and working less, when do you think would be the best time to start?

Go ahead and go to BrainshareByJoe.com and set up a consultation with me. The conversation is free. Even if we don't work together, my goal is to give you an actionable, clear plan to increase your sales and profits and reduce the number of hours you work.

Also, if you found this book valuable, at least contact my office and I'll send you some extra copies of this book that you can give to your networking contacts. Do you think any of your business contacts could benefit from this book?

Congratulations, you are well on your way to building a successful business that provides you enough money and time to live on your own terms. I'll talk to you soon.

Joe Siecinski

Joe Siecinski

About The Author

Joe Siecinski is a certified business coach. He has spent over 25 years in sales, marketing, and management as a Fortune 50 executive. He holds a Bachelor's degree in engineering and an MBA in marketing and is an NLP practitioner. He has worked with over 1500 clients and has done over 2000 face-to-face sales calls.

He lives in the San Francisco Bay Area with his wife and son.

Working with Joe has been extremely helpful to my business. Three things stand out: 1) The calendaring system he teaches works. I've tried quite a few and found most to be a burden. This works for me. 2) His ability to pose questions that cause you to look at things from another angle. 3) His sincerity in wanting to help you to be enormously successful. I started as a skeptic. Now I'm a fan.

Dave Kocharhook
Senior Vice President at Midland American Capital

There are consultants and there are coaches, and then there's Joe Siecinski. And he's not just big on theory. He has the experience, the technical savvy, and the tools to make sure that, whatever challenges you face in your business, you see them as opportunities, and he's there with you as you get in there and get it done.

Joe has made a big difference in my small business. Think what a difference he can make in your larger business! He's enthusiastic, thoughtful, and persistent. He follows up and he follows through. I cannot recommend him highly enough.

Meg Dastrup
Meg Dastrup's Word Power Plus
Santa Clara, CA

I met Joe around six months ago by pure chance. It's been a wonderful journey since then. He has helped me organize my business life and get more time back in my day. Joe's greatest value to the business community and families is his business calendaring system. Before using his system, I worked a full 50 hour week, with no results. But when i did the test, turns out I was just doing 15 hours a week of productive work. I certainly haven't meet anyone working building a large business working 4 hours a week but I have meet successful people using Joe's calendaring system. I rate it as one of the vital tools for launching a new business.

Prudhvi T.
San Jose, CA

I really enjoyed working with Joe. I love fast paced material and moving through things at a rapid pace. He picked up on this within the first 10 minutes of our discussion and adapted our discussion to give me heaps of information quickly. That style of quick adaptation was prevalent in all of our coaching conversations.

Joe also had incredible background and knowledge to draw from. He does quite a bit of work focused on small businesses, and I can see why. Many people in this space need help in sales and marketing as well as prioritizing the difficult, vague, and challenging tasks they face. This is exactly where Joe excels.

My personal recommendation is the time management and calendaring system Joe teaches is absolutely phenomenal. I consider myself to be pretty good at time management already and have been a subscriber to the 'Getting Things Done' philosophy for quite some time. Joe brings some additional crucial elements into this framework that don't take much time, but add tremendous value.

My advice would be to go see him for a single session. If it's not a fit, you'll know immediately. If it is, you've got your business success to gain.

Travis M.
Palo Alto, CA

Joe is an experienced and dynamic marketing professional. He is also a tenacious, enthusiastic, and focused business coach that will get you results in your business.

David Gazave
Certified Executive Business Coach

Joe is a fantastic business coach. He has a wealth of expertise to share. When we first met, we outlined what exactly I wanted to achieve with our time together. He put together a strategy for our sessions, based on MY specific needs. I've been seeing great results since the very first session. I can't recommend Joe more highly!

Elyse T.
Alameda, CA

I have been working with Joe for several months now and the progress towards my business goals have never been clearer. He has saved me considerable time clarifying how to be of greatest value to clients and customers. I strongly suggest anyone that is trying to get their business to the next level contact Joe. He will rapidly help you to focus on results that matter for your business and your customers.

Stuart Levin, MBA
Franchise Education Executive

WOW, Joe has a great way of giving you the structure step by step to improve my business. His way of teaching and coaching me has given the confidence that I needed to accomplish more and his knowledge of how it can be done is nothing short of Great. In the last two months, he has enabled me to plan, implement, and accomplish things that were stressing before. Joe has guided me in a way that no other person has been able to and given me the guidelines to look at my business in a whole new way. I do not have any hesitation in recommending and am planning to continue using this great asset of knowledge that he has.

George L.
Milpitas, CA

Joe teaches you how to be an intelligent business owner, and he does it custom-tailored to you and your business. My business' most urgent challenge was marketing and sales. Within the first 30 days of taking up Joe's services, I was able to close the biggest long-term contract my company has made in its 2 years. Along with the technical knowledge of marketing/sales, he instills a confidence in you through his teaching to help you carry out the tasks that need to be done to make your business successful.

HIGHLY RECOMMENDED and INCREDIBLY FUN TO WORK WITH!!!!

Palli S.
Sunnyvale, CA

Working with Joe requires you to think about your business in a whole new way. And that's not a bad thing. While we don't like looking at certain parts of our business, Joe makes it easy because he's neither pushy or mean. He makes it safe to learn what you don't know and fix your problems. Joe is intense and hilarious which is really helpful when you're getting stressed about running your business. Joe's passion is so helpful and he's on the same journey as other business owners, understanding what it's like to walk in our shoes.

Hire him.

Anne K.
San Mateo, CA

Joe has been a great coach. After meeting with him for the first time, we put some business strategies together and I had had my best month ever! I look forward to working with Joe in the future. He is knowledgeable, personable and wants to see you grow!

Jeff R.
San Jose, CA

I had the most amazing meeting with Joe today. My marketing plan materialized as if from a deep steeping fog. Not only did I find clarity, I found focus and confidence. I have met many coaches, I have been consulting for a long time, but this is the first time I have worked with a coach for my business and I am hooked!

Zoe S.
Mill Valley, CA

Joe is a great coach and mentor. He is extremely knowledgeable in sales and marketing techniques, and helps people develop a technique suited to their personality. So, it really works. He has made a difference in my approach towards my business and all for the better.

Sarada M.,
San Jose, CA

Joe Siecinski is my coach for few months now. He has amazing patience. He listens well and adjusts to your needs and style extremely well. He gives all the time I need.

I have not had a coach before so I was reluctant to get one. Hence, I attended his 90-day business planning workshop to get to know his style first. I was blown away with the details around business plan required for planning your business success.

I received individual coaching on weekly basis. And now I am in ProfitClub. What a wonderful group of people in the group. I appreciate the ability to mastermind ideas with my peers!

Coaching does work! Thank you, Coach Joe!

Madan A.
San Jose, CA

I've worked with Joe off and on for the past year or so and have had spectacular results. Joe is a business coach but in reality his coaching touches all aspects of your life. Joe has helped me with time management, goal setting, and has given me several new ideas for running and marketing my business. Last year Joe helped me grow my business by double digit percentages! Joe is a great guy and I highly recommend him.

Ravinder Lal.
San Jose, CA

I met Joe at a networking event and signed up for

his introductory session. It was awesome! Joe is really committed to helping business owners, and that really came across throughout the session. He offered very constructive criticism that frankly, wasn't all the pleasant to hear, but I know I needed it and I really appreciate the honesty and truthfulness. After all, as a small business owner, working on your business means working on yourself. Had another session with him today that went deep into those areas where I need improvement. Practice, practice, practice! I highly recommend Joe as a business coach for honest, practical skills that could only take your business further.

Elizabeth G.
San Francisco, CA

To schedule a free consultation with Joe, go to
BrainshareByJoe.com.

To request more copies of this book, or to get printed or
digital copies of the worksheets and planners presented
in this book, go to BrainshareByJoe.com

Joe Siecinski

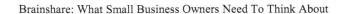

Publishing, production, and editing by Valenzuela Press.

Joe Siecinski

Made in the USA
Lexington, KY
04 November 2019

56461589R00048